PENGUIN
ENGLISH TESTS

BOOK 5

Jake Allsop

PENGUIN ENGLISH

PENGUIN BOOKS

Published by the Penguin Group
Penguin Books Ltd, 27 Wrights Lane, London W8 5TZ, England
Viking Penguin, a division of Penguin Books USA Inc.,
375 Hudson Street, New York, New York 10014, USA
Penguin Books Australia Ltd, Ringwood, Victoria, Australia
Penguin Books Canada Ltd, 2801 John Street, Markham, Ontario, Canada L3R 1B4
Penguin Books (NZ) Ltd, 182–190 Wairau Road, Auckland 10, New Zealand

Penguin Books Ltd, Registered Offices: Harmondsworth, Middlesex, England

First published 1991
1 3 5 7 9 10 8 6 4 2

Designed by Jacky Wedgwood
Illustrations by James Val/Joan Farmer Artists

Set in Linotron 202 10/11pt Bembo

Made and printed in Great Britain by
BPCC Hazell Books
Aylesbury, Bucks, England
Member of BPCC Ltd.

CONTENTS

Acknowledgements

We thank the following patient and long-suffering people and institutions, and their students, for their generous help in field-testing the material:

Rachel Belgrave and Ms de Vivier (Regent School, London, UK); Sue Evans and colleagues (King's School, Bournemouth, UK); Richard French (York House, Barcelona, Spain); Kathy Gude and colleagues (Barnet College, UK); Paul Johnston and colleagues (Regent School, Brighton, UK); Janet Simms, John Cooke and colleagues (King's College, Bournemouth, UK); Sara Smyth and colleagues (Hendon College, UK); Janet Blake, Ken Erickson, Jackie Godfrey, Marion Heron, Şadiye Behçetoğulları, Feliş Besbelli, Meltem Çağlayam, Meral Guçeri, Selim Karabıyık and Ayşen Tosya of Busel, Bilkent University, Ankara, Turkey; Peter Watcyn-Jones and Vanda Lilja, Steve Myers, Jane Myers, Sue Sembo, Alison Gilling, Sharon Ingleson, Rose Reddy (Folkuniversitetet in Malmö and Lund, Sweden); Beth Williams and colleagues (Liceo Internazionale, Milan, Italy).

Thanks go also to Joy McKellen and Van Milne for their help in steering the project and for their many useful comments and suggestions.

INTRODUCTION

Purpose of the tests

These multiple-choice tests are designed to assess students' progress during courses of study from upper-intermediate to advanced level, corresponding roughly to the Cambridge Advanced English or Proficiency. The language items are derived from an analysis of commonly used course-books at this level, including Cassell's *Foundation English* and Longman's *Kernel* series, as well as a range of pre-CPE and CPE coursebooks. This battery of tests has been produced for a wide range of teaching situations and has been extensively field-tested both in the UK and overseas.

Each book contains ten tests of forty items each. Within each book there are three levels of language difficulty and three alternative or parallel tests for each level. The tenth test in each book, called the Review Test, is designed to function as an achievement test.

LEVEL ONE	LEVEL TWO	LEVEL THREE	ACHIEVEMENT
Test 1	Test 1	Test 1	
Test 2	Test 2	Test 2	Review Test
Test 3	Test 3	Test 3	

The teacher's notes to each book contain:

- a distribution list showing the kind of language items being tested; this can be used for diagnostic purposes;
- an inventory of the language items;
- a key to the tests.

Level of the tests

Teaching systems vary widely. As a rough guide, the level of the book is equivalent to 450–600 hours of teaching. By the end of the teaching corresponding to this book, students would typically be at a level to pass the Cambridge Advanced English or Proficiency examinations or equivalent.

Distribution of items

The structure of each test is as follows:

ITEM NO.   LANGUAGE AREA

1–15   Testing for grammatical accuracy
    1–4   Tenses
    5   Conjunctions
    6   Irregular verbs
    7–10   Prepositional uses
    11–12 Verbs in collocations
    13–15 Phrasal verbs

16–25   Testing knowledge of vocabulary
    16–20 Word selection (e.g., near synonyms, false friends)
    21–25 Idiomatic expressions

26–30   Testing knowledge of word building
    26–30 Common prefixes and suffixes

31–35   Testing ability in reading comprehension
    31–35 Comprehension items based on edited extracts from *The Penguin Book of Very Short Stories*

36–40   Testing knowledge of phonological features
    36–38 Phonemic distinctions
    39–40 Word stress

Administration of the tests

Field-testing of both single- and mixed-nationality groups in the UK and overseas suggests that each test, excluding preliminary administrative tasks such as issuing test books and going through instructions, will take between forty and forty-five minutes.

A note on 'correct' answers

It is tiresome for teachers to be faced with the argument that one of the distractors is also 'possible'. For example, a 'possible' response to an introductory 'My name is John Smith' is 'Your humble servant, sir', but it is many decades since that response was current. The criteria for judging the 'correctness' of an answer are:

1 Does it conform to the norm of English being taught? Thus, a feature that is acceptable in American English must be 'correct' if the English being taught is American English, even though it would not be the preferred form for a British teacher. We have tried to avoid such distractors.

2 If the answer satisfies the first criterion, is it then acceptable? A form that is theoretically possible may be unacceptable because it is not

idiomatic, that is, it is not the usual or preferred form of a native English speaker. This criterion would eliminate archaisms like 'Your humble servant' or unacceptable variants like 'start from the scratch' instead of 'start from scratch'.

Inventory of language items in Book 5

STRUCTURAL ITEMS

bound to do something; daresay; defining and non-defining relatives; didn't need to vs. needn't have; doesn't bear doing; have something done; high/about time + past; inversion in conditionals (e.g., Had I = If I had); modals: compound tenses; modals: non-finite forms; must/can't do/be doing; negative inversion with scarcely/no sooner, only; passive constructions (e.g., is said to be, to have/having been done); compound passives; rather not + base infinitive; should you = if you happen to; tenses after is/was as if; will you do vs. will you be doing; would = used to; would like/have liked to do/have done something.

CONJUNCTIONS

as long as = providing; however hard; much as; now that; once = after; or else; seeing that; such that; while = although.

IRREGULAR VERBS

bid, breed, burst, cling, creep, deal, dwell, fling, flow, forbid, forecast, forego, forsake, freeze, hang, hit, kneel, mow, quit, rid, ring, sew, sing, sit, sleep, slit, sow, spit, split, sting, string, thrust, tread, upset, weave, weep, wring, write.

PREPOSITIONS

abide by, abstain from, account for, allergic to, apart from, at your best, by virtue of, confined to, dawn on, deny Ø doing, dispose of, elaborate on, emphasise Ø, exempt from, handy for, impact on, in the lead, inoculate against, irrespective of, on good terms, over a given time, peculiar to, plough through, prone to, pry into, recall Ø, refrain from, rely on, remind somebody of, reminiscent of, resist Ø doing, something of your own, side with, specialise in, take pride in, under no circumstances, under pressure, vouch for, within a given time.

COLLOCATIONS

bat an eyelid; beat about the bush; bend over backwards; bite off more than you can chew; bite somebody's head off; cry over spilt milk; draw the line; follow in somebody's footsteps; follow suit; knock somebody down with a feather; land on your feet; make ends meet; not lift a finger; not miss a trick; pay lip service; play your cards; set somebody's mind at rest; spread like wildfire; start from scratch; stick out (like a sore thumb).

Phrasal verb with adverbial particle: blend in; brush up; crop up; die out; drop off = fall asleep; go off (of a gun); let off = explode; pass away = die; press on; tone down. Phrasal verb with adverbial particle and preposition: catch up with, check up on, come up with, cut down on, fall behind with, get around to, get away with, get down to, go down with, go in for, go on about, grow out of, keep up with, look back on, put in for, speak out against, stand up for, stick out for, tune in to, walk out on somebody.

VOCABULARY

Word selection: amenity/convenience, attribute/prescribe, before long, broad/bright (daylight), clutch/grasp, consistent/consequent, diversion/deviation, drip/drop, enable/approve, enterprising/initiative, fair/honest, fit/well, glimpse/glance, glow/glare, grounds/causes, in the long run, jeer/clap, let alone, minutes/protocol, nick of time, pat/stroke, poster/propaganda, precise/accurate, pretentious/precious, procedure/process, prolific/generous, rank/grade, recollection/memory, review/commentary, roaring/burning, shape/build, skid/skate, slaughter/decimate, slip of the tongue, slot/slit, spell/while, stripe/stroke, stumble/stammer, stutter/stagger, swear/testify, the spur of the moment, tip/peak, toss/throw, track/road, trudge/stroll, unscrupulous/depraved, utterly/perfectly, warn/prevent, withdraw/remove.

Idioms: a stone's throw, back to square one, bark up the wrong tree, be out of your depth, benefit of the doubt, by the skin of your teeth, chip on your shoulder, come to terms with, cost the earth, do something by the book, do your level best, eleventh hour, flying visit, for the life of me, get cold feet, get hold of the wrong end of the stick, get the hang of something, give something a miss, go out like a light, go to pieces, hit the roof, keep your wits about you, know something like the back of your hand, know where you stand with somebody, lion's share, load off your mind, narrow escape, not sleep a wink, off the cuff, off the record, out of the blue, pain in the neck, pay your respects, put your cards on the table, put your foot in it, rest on your laurels, rule of thumb, save something for a rainy day, short of = apart from, square peg in a round hole, stick your neck out, sweep somebody off his/her feet, take the bull by the horns, talk shop, the crack of dawn, the last straw, think better of something, value for money, vanish into thin air, vicious circle.

WORD BUILDING

Affixes im-/ir-; -ful and -less; negative affix dis-. Word formation using suffixes -al, -ance, -ety, -ence, -hood, -ion, -(i)ty, -ness, -ship, -ure, -y, Ø change.

PHONOLOGY

Various graphemic/phonemic contrasts. Stress in polysyllabic words: administrative, arithmetical, characteristic, conspiratorial, deliberately, extraordinary, ostentatiously, particularly, prejudicial, superstitious.

Words with two pronunciations and a change of meaning: advocate, alternate, appropriate, approximate, articulate, associate, bow, coordinate, degenerate, delegate, deliberate, elaborate, estimate, excuse, graduate, house, intimate, lead, live, minute, moderate, row, separate, sow, tear, use, wind, wound.

LEVEL ONE

TEST 1

A *Grammar*

> *Choose the correct answer. Only one answer is correct.*
>
> EXAMPLE: Hurry up! The train ☐ A was   here shortly
>
>   ☐ B has been
>
>   ☐ C is
>
>   ☐ D will be
>
> *The correct answer is* D: 'will be'.

1 You must ☐ A have been tired if you had fallen   asleep in the train

          ☐ B be tired if you had fallen

          ☐ C have been tired if you fell

          ☐ D have been tired if you fall

2 Isn't it about time you ☐ A took   your coat off?

                  ☐ B take

                  ☐ C will take

                  ☐ D are taking

3 Scarcely ☐ A he arrived   when the fight broke out

        ☐ B he had arrived

        ☐ C did he arrive

        ☐ D had he arrived

4 Which sentence is closest in meaning to the sentence underlined?
<u>He didn't need to go to London</u>

  ☐ A He went to London because he wanted to

  ☐ B He wasn't obliged to go to London

  ☐ C He didn't go to London because it wasn't necessary

  ☐ D He went to London even though it wasn't necessary

5 You can borrow the car ☐ A while ⠀⠀⠀you promise to drive
⠀⠀⠀⠀⠀⠀⠀⠀⠀⠀⠀⠀⠀☐ B as long as ⠀carefully
⠀⠀⠀⠀⠀⠀⠀⠀⠀⠀⠀⠀⠀☐ C so that
⠀⠀⠀⠀⠀⠀⠀⠀⠀⠀⠀⠀⠀☐ D for

6 Three of these verbs have different forms for infinitive, past tense and
past participle, like speak – spoke – spoken. Which one does not?

☐ A mow ⠀☐ B sow ⠀☐ C flow ⠀☐ D sew

7 George is the sort of man you can always rely ☐ A to ⠀⠀in a crisis
⠀⠀⠀⠀⠀⠀⠀⠀⠀⠀⠀⠀⠀⠀⠀⠀⠀⠀⠀⠀⠀⠀☐ B for
⠀⠀⠀⠀⠀⠀⠀⠀⠀⠀⠀⠀⠀⠀⠀⠀⠀⠀⠀⠀⠀⠀☐ C with
⠀⠀⠀⠀⠀⠀⠀⠀⠀⠀⠀⠀⠀⠀⠀⠀⠀⠀⠀⠀⠀⠀☐ D on

8 I can never resist ☐ A from ⠀⠀talking about other people's love lives
⠀⠀⠀⠀⠀⠀⠀⠀⠀⠀⠀☐ B –
⠀⠀⠀⠀⠀⠀⠀⠀⠀⠀⠀☐ C against
⠀⠀⠀⠀⠀⠀⠀⠀⠀⠀⠀☐ D of

9 This isn't a very nice house, but it is really handy ☐ A of ⠀⠀the station
⠀⠀⠀⠀⠀⠀⠀⠀⠀⠀⠀⠀⠀⠀⠀⠀⠀⠀⠀⠀⠀⠀⠀⠀⠀⠀☐ B for
⠀⠀⠀⠀⠀⠀⠀⠀⠀⠀⠀⠀⠀⠀⠀⠀⠀⠀⠀⠀⠀⠀⠀⠀⠀⠀☐ C to
⠀⠀⠀⠀⠀⠀⠀⠀⠀⠀⠀⠀⠀⠀⠀⠀⠀⠀⠀⠀⠀⠀⠀⠀⠀⠀☐ D by

10 You can get a free ticket irrespective ☐ A of ⠀⠀how old you are
⠀⠀⠀⠀⠀⠀⠀⠀⠀⠀⠀⠀⠀⠀⠀⠀⠀⠀⠀⠀⠀⠀☐ B –
⠀⠀⠀⠀⠀⠀⠀⠀⠀⠀⠀⠀⠀⠀⠀⠀⠀⠀⠀⠀⠀⠀☐ C for
⠀⠀⠀⠀⠀⠀⠀⠀⠀⠀⠀⠀⠀⠀⠀⠀⠀⠀⠀⠀⠀⠀☐ D to

11 When you are playing cards, you are expected to ☐ A hold ⠀⠀suit
⠀⠀⠀⠀⠀⠀⠀⠀⠀⠀⠀⠀⠀⠀⠀⠀⠀⠀⠀⠀⠀⠀⠀⠀⠀⠀☐ B obey
⠀⠀⠀⠀⠀⠀⠀⠀⠀⠀⠀⠀⠀⠀⠀⠀⠀⠀⠀⠀⠀⠀⠀⠀⠀⠀☐ C follow
⠀⠀⠀⠀⠀⠀⠀⠀⠀⠀⠀⠀⠀⠀⠀⠀⠀⠀⠀⠀⠀⠀⠀⠀⠀⠀☐ D copy

12 Don't worry about me. I'm like a cat: I always ☐ A land   on my feet

        ☐ B stand

        ☐ C jump

        ☐ D stay

13 The gun ☐ A hit   off without warning

    ☐ B blew

    ☐ C went

    ☐ D drew

14 I intend to steal the Crown Jewels.

    You'll never get ☐ A up to   it!

        ☐ B out of

        ☐ C in on

        ☐ D away with

15 You'll be in trouble when the examinations come, if you fall

    ☐ A behind with   your work

    ☐ B out of

    ☐ C away from

    ☐ D down to

B *Vocabulary*

Choose the correct answer. Only one answer is correct.

EXAMPLE: How long did it ☐ A take   you to knit that scarf?

        ☐ B need

        ☐ C bring

        ☐ D make

The correct answer is A: 'take'.

16 It is easy for cars to ☐ A skate   on wet roads after a dry spell

        ☐ B slither

        ☐ C skid

        ☐ D slip

17 What is the ☐ A precise   difference between a butterfly and a moth?

     ☐ B accurate

     ☐ C correct

     ☐ D very

18 We weren't sure where to go for our honeymoon. We decided on

     Mauritius on the ☐ A heat   of the moment

     ☐ B spur

     ☐ C urge

     ☐ D push

19 Apart from a few bad ☐ A commentaries   , most critics liked his new

     ☐ B summaries   book

     ☐ C values

     ☐ D reviews

20 There has been an accident on the motorway. Motorists are advised to

     look out for ☐ A bypass   signs

     ☐ B deviation

     ☐ C diversion

     ☐ D roundabout

21 I could not for the ☐ A rest   of me remember his name

     ☐ B worth

     ☐ C life

     ☐ D hope

22 Your new car must have cost ☐ A an eye

     ☐ B the earth

     ☐ C a bank

     ☐ D a leg

23 He seemed to go ☐ A to pieces   after his friend's death

     ☐ B to rack and ruin

     ☐ C by the board

     ☐ D down and out

24 Don't worry if you can't do it first time.

You'll soon ☐ A see the light   of it

☐ B have a way

☐ C get the hang

☐ D make the best

25 Paul sold everything he owned and went to live in Tahiti. Without

warning, ☐ A out of the blue

☐ B off the cuff

☐ C like a flash in the pan

☐ D once in a blue moon

C *Word building*

Choose the ending which forms a noun related to the word given. Only one ending is correct.

EXAMPLE: explain

☐ A expla–   -inment

☐ B expla–   -nation

☐ C expla–   -inure

☐ D expla–   -nity

The answer is B: 'explanation'.

26 Choose the ending which forms a noun related to the word 'hard'.

☐ A hard–   -liness

☐ B hard–   -hood

☐ C hard–   -ship

☐ D hard–   -ery

27 Choose the ending which forms a noun related to the word 'boy'.

☐ A boy–   -dom

☐ B boy–   -hood

☐ C boy–   -ness

☐ D boy–   -ety

28 Three of these adjectives make their opposite by adding the prefix im-, e.g., mutable → immutable. Find the one that does not.

☐ A modest   ☐ B movable   ☐ C moderate   ☐ D manageable

29 Only one of these adjectives can be changed to another by changing -ful to -less, e.g., hopeful to hopeless. Which one is it?

☐ A careful   ☐ B peaceful   ☐ C successful   ☐ D grateful

30 Three of these words make their opposite by adding the prefix dis-, e.g., reputable → disreputable. Find the one that does not.

☐ A respectful   ☐ B agreeable   ☐ C interested   ☐ D truthful

D Reading comprehension

Fill in the gaps in the passage with the words which make sense.

EXAMPLE:

If you have broken both your legs, [1] _____ on a skiing holiday.
After all, [2] _____ much fun just watching others enjoying
themselves on the ski slopes.

[1] ☐ A everyone enjoys going

☐ B what a good idea it would be to go

☐ C why don't you go

☐ D there's not much point in going

The answer is D: 'there's not much point in going'.

[2] ☐ A what would be

☐ B you wouldn't have

☐ C you could have

☐ D there would be

The answer is B: 'you wouldn't have'.

Fred lived alone, his wife having died a year or two before. He [31] _____
middle-aged, not handsome but with a pleasant face that seemed to
encourage women to confide in him. He was good at it because [32] _____
actually get on well with women. Of course, most men will tell you, and
themselves, that they like women, but [33] _____ most men feel more

comfortable [34] _____ other men. They *need* women, certainly, as lovers and mothers and housekeepers and admirers, but on the whole [35] _____, probably because they do not really understand them.

31 ☐ A was still no more than
   ☐ B had not quite reached
   ☐ C didn't look a bit like
   ☐ D thought that by the time he was

32 ☐ A there was nothing for it but to
   ☐ B it was easy for him
   ☐ C he was one of those rare men who
   ☐ D of his unusual talent for

33 ☐ A the truth of the matter
   ☐ B the fact is that
   ☐ C it's a question of
   ☐ D the result is that

34 ☐ A by the side of
   ☐ B when it comes to
   ☐ C to spend little time with
   ☐ D in the company of

35 ☐ A most men get on well with women
   ☐ B they do not actually like them
   ☐ C women get the worst of it
   ☐ D husbands treat their wives badly

E *Phonology*

In three of the four words, the underlined part is pronounced in the same way. Find the other word, in which the underlined part is pronounced differently.

EXAMPLE: ☐ A l<u>ear</u>n   ☐ B b<u>ir</u>d   ☐ C h<u>ear</u>t   ☐ D w<u>or</u>th

The answer is C: 'heart'.

36 ☐ A anal<u>y</u>sis ☐ B magnif<u>i</u>cent ☐ C consi<u>d</u>erate ☐ D tri<u>f</u>le

37 ☐ A <u>wh</u>ile ☐ B <u>wh</u>ole ☐ C <u>wh</u>o ☐ D <u>wh</u>ose

38 ☐ A s<u>u</u>gar ☐ B b<u>u</u>tcher ☐ C st<u>u</u>mble ☐ D c<u>u</u>shion

39 Where does the stress fall in the word 'particularly'?

☐ A   ☐ B ☐ C ☐ D ☐ E
part   ic   ul   ar   ly

40 Three of these words can be pronounced in two different ways with a change of meaning, e.g., the verb 'to graduate' [gradu–eit], and the noun 'a graduate' [gradu –ɐt]. Find the other word, which can be pronounced in only one way.

☐ A intimate ☐ B celebrate ☐ C articulate ☐ D advocate

LEVEL ONE

TEST 2

A *Grammar*

> *Choose the correct answer. Only one answer is correct.*
>
> EXAMPLE: Hurry up! The train ☐ A was   here shortly
>
>   ☐ B has been
>
>   ☐ C is
>
>   ☐ D will be
>
> *The correct answer is* D: 'will be'.

1 You must ☐ A be starving by the time you get   to York

        ☐ B be starving by the time you had got

        ☐ C have been starving by the time you got

        ☐ D have been starving by the time you get

2 It's high time you ☐ A went

               ☐ B for you to go

               ☐ C that you go

               ☐ D for you going

3 ☐ A We scarcely   started eating when there was another
    scream

   ☐ B We had scarcely

   ☐ C We scarcely had

   ☐ D Scarcely we

4 Which sentence is closest in meaning to the sentence underlined?
I daresay he made his money from illegal activities

    ☐ A I think he was a crook and I'm not afraid to say so

    ☐ B I think it is quite likely that he was a crook

    ☐ C I have heard people say that he was a crook

    ☐ D I don't really believe that he was a crook

5 ☐ A Seen   that you have worked so hard, you can take
   ☐ B In view   tomorrow off
   ☐ C Just now
   ☐ D Seeing

6 Three of these verbs have the same form for infinitive, past tense and past participle, i.e., they are like put – put – put. Which one does not?

☐ A thrust ☐ B trust ☐ C burst ☐ D upset

7 You remind me ☐ A of   my Aunt's parrot when you talk like that
   ☐ B –
   ☐ C for
   ☐ D about

8 Would you like to elaborate ☐ A with   your last answer?
   ☐ B over
   ☐ C about
   ☐ D on

9 Everybody finished early apart ☐ A –   Melanie
   ☐ B of
   ☐ C from
   ☐ D for

10 She always seems to work better when she is ☐ A on   pressure
   ☐ B under
   ☐ C in
   ☐ D with

11 We've never done anything like it before. We'll have to
   ☐ A make a   scratch
   ☐ B start from
   ☐ C draw the
   ☐ D give some

12 He's ☐ A following   in his father's footsteps

☐ B copying

☐ C stepping

☐ D hanging

13 To avoid talking about dying, we say that someone

☐ A fell   away

☐ B went

☐ C slipped

☐ D passed

14 You go ahead, I'll catch ☐ A on to   you later

☐ B out on

☐ C up with

☐ D down on

15 Don't let your brother bully you. Stand ☐ A in for   him

☐ B up above

☐ C away from

☐ D up to

B *Vocabulary*

Choose the correct answer. Only one answer is correct.

EXAMPLE: How long did it ☐ A take   you to knit that scarf?

☐ B need

☐ C bring

☐ D make

The correct answer is A: 'take'.

16 It was just a ☐ A fault   of the tongue
                ☐ B lapse
                ☐ C slip
                ☐ D miss

17 If you are a vegetarian, you should give up eggs and milk as well as meat
if you want to be ☐ A consequent
                  ☐ B consistent
                  ☐ C constant
                  ☐ D logic

18 We were just about to give your seat to someone else: you got here
in the ☐ A nick   of time
        ☐ B second
        ☐ C split
        ☐ D point

19 The secretary read out the ☐ A minutes   of the last meeting
                        ☐ B protocol
                        ☐ C formulas
                        ☐ D records

20 I'm afraid we shall have to ☐ A dismiss   with your services
                      ☐ B discharge
                      ☐ C dispense
                      ☐ D discount

21 The prototype failed for the third time. Once again it looks as if we are
back to ☐ A number   one, I'm afraid
        ☐ B square
        ☐ C part
        ☐ D line

22 I was so exhausted that I went out like a ☐ A light
☐ B baby
☐ C candle
☐ D log

23 He isn't very tactful, but at least you know
☐ A what's the time   with him
☐ B where you stand
☐ C who's who
☐ D how it goes

24 He's finding it very hard to ☐ A do away with   his brother's
☐ B make a go of   death
☐ C get the better of
☐ D come to terms with

25 He is a very cautious man. He likes to do everything ☐ A for the best
☐ B in principle
☐ C by the book
☐ D off the cuff

C Word building

Choose the ending which forms a noun related to the word given. Only one ending is correct.

EXAMPLE: explain
☐ A expla- -inment
☐ B expla- -nation
☐ C expla- -inure
☐ D expla- -nity

The answer is B: 'explanation'.

26 Choose the ending which forms a noun related to the word 'trivial'.

☐ A trivia- -lity

☐ B trivia- -tion

☐ C trivia- -lry

☐ D trivia- -nce

27 Choose the ending which forms a noun related to the word 'despair'.

☐ A desp- -arity

☐ B desp- -erance

☐ C desp- -eration

☐ D desp- -airment

28 Three of these words make their opposite by adding the prefix im-, e.g. mutable → immutable. Find the one that does not.

☐ A moral ☐ B pleasant ☐ C mortal ☐ D patient

29 Only one of these words can be changed to another by changing -ful to -less, e.g., hopeful to hopeless. Which one is it?

☐ A resentful ☐ B dreadful ☐ C spiteful ☐ D mindful

30 Three of these words make their opposite by adding the prefix dis-, e.g., reputable → disreputable. Find the one that does not.

☐ A promote ☐ B approve ☐ C connect ☐ D like

D Reading comprehension

Fill in the gaps in the passage with the words which make sense.

EXAMPLE:

If you have broken both your legs, [1] _____ on a skiing holiday. After all, [2] _____ much fun just watching others enjoying themselves on the ski slopes.

[1] ☐ A everyone enjoys going

☐ B what a good idea it would be to go

☐ C why don't you go

☐ D there's not much point in going

The answer is D: 'there's not much point in going'.

[2] ☐ A what would be

    ☐ B you wouldn't have

    ☐ C you could have

    ☐ D there would be

The answer is B: 'you wouldn't have'.

Fred enjoyed the company of women, and he understood them. He knew
[31] _____ married women to look after houses and husbands and children,
[32] _____ serve up perhaps twenty meals a week and to nurse the family
through its problems and illnesses. And then when their husbands came
home in the evening, their wives had to listen patiently while they
complained about the boss or the terrible time [33] _____ that day. And
[34] _____, these same women were trying to stay attractive and lively.
Fred understood all this, and [35] _____ to his married ladies.

31 ☐ A how many times a week

    ☐ B everything there was to know about

    ☐ C that life was not easy for

    ☐ D what it was like for

32 ☐ A not to mention

    ☐ B day after day

    ☐ C when it came to

    ☐ D having to

33 ☐ A they had had at work

    ☐ B it was for them

    ☐ C they took the journey home

    ☐ D to work like slaves

34 ☐ A it made no difference

    ☐ B all the time

    ☐ C while he was listening to them

    ☐ D so far as the family was concerned

35 ☐ A spent a lot of his time

    ☐ B tried to spare their lives

    ☐ C did his best to be a good friend

    ☐ D never wanted to leave it all behind

E *Phonology*

In three of the four words, the underlined part is pronounced in the same way. Find the other word, in which the underlined part is pronounced differently.

EXAMPLE: ☐ A le<u>ar</u>n ☐ B b<u>ir</u>d ☐ C h<u>ear</u>t ☐ D w<u>or</u>th

The answer is C: 'heart'.

36 ☐ A h<u>a</u>sty ☐ B n<u>a</u>sty ☐ C t<u>a</u>sty ☐ D w<u>a</u>stage

37 ☐ A sei<u>z</u>ure ☐ B mea<u>s</u>ure ☐ C confu<u>s</u>ion ☐ D ten<u>s</u>ion

38 ☐ A dist<u>ri</u>bute ☐ B t<u>ri</u>be ☐ C t<u>ri</u>angle ☐ D t<u>ri</u>al

39 Where does the stress fall in the word 'conspiratorial'?

    ☐ A   ☐ B   ☐ C   ☐ D   ☐ E
    con   spir   at   or   ial

40 Three of these words can be pronounced in two different ways with a change of meaning, e.g., the verb 'to graduate' [gradu-eit], and the noun 'a graduate' [gradu -ɕt]. Find the other word, which can be pronounced in only one way.

    ☐ A coordinate ☐ B degenerate ☐ C deliberate ☐ D speculate

LEVEL ONE

TEST 3

A *Grammar*

> *Choose the correct answer. Only one answer is correct.*
>
> EXAMPLE: Hurry up! The train ☐ A was   here shortly
>
>   ☐ B has been
>
>   ☐ C is
>
>   ☐ D will be
>
> *The correct answer is* D: 'will be'.

1 It ☐ A couldn't be too hard if you are   able to finish it in an
     ☐ B can't have been too hard if you had been   hour
     ☐ C can't have been too hard if you were
     ☐ D couldn't be too hard if you had been

2 ☐ A It's time   you put your toys away
     ☐ B There's time
     ☐ C It's the time
     ☐ D There is a time

3 It was only then ☐ A did I realise   how much I owed to her
     ☐ B had I realised
     ☐ C I did realise
     ☐ D that I realised

4 Which sentence is closest in meaning to the sentence underlined?
She's bound to see Harry at the meeting

     ☐ A She is obliged to see Harry at the meeting

     ☐ B She is on her way to see Harry at the meeting

     ☐ C It is certain that she will see Harry at the meeting

     ☐ D She's tied up, and too busy to see Harry at the meeting

5 Put that knife down ☐ A then if not   I'll call the police!

☐ B or else

☐ C other than

☐ D besides

6 Three of these verbs have different forms for infinitive, past tense and past participle, like speak – spoke – spoken. Which one does not?

☐ A forbid   ☐ B forsake   ☐ C forecast   ☐ D forego

7 Please refrain ☐ A from   smoking until you are in the terminal building

☐ B of

☐ C –

☐ D for

8 For the sake of other passengers, please abstain ☐ A from   smoking cigars

☐ B to

☐ C of

☐ D on

9 You seem to be ☐ A at   very good terms with your ex-wife

☐ B in

☐ C under

☐ D on

10 This place is reminiscent ☐ A for   Vienna

☐ B of

☐ C in

☐ D about

11 You've got to ☐ A set   the line somewhere

☐ B make

☐ C draw

☐ D cross

12 They are so poor, I don't know how they manage to make ends

☐ A fasten

☐ B touch

☐ C join

☐ D meet

13 I need to ☐ A tart   up my French. It's years since I studied it

☐ B brush

☐ C smooth

☐ D tune

14 Old soldiers love to reminisce, to look ☐ A back on   their army

☐ B up at   days

☐ C away from

☐ D forward to

15 Amnesty International speaks ☐ A up for   injustice wherever it

☐ B out against   finds it

☐ C in on

☐ D down on

B *Vocabulary*

Choose the correct answer. Only one answer is correct.

EXAMPLE: How long did it ☐ A take   you to knit that scarf?

☐ B need

☐ C bring

☐ D make

The correct answer is A: 'take'.

16 Look at the car with the black ☐ A stroke   down the side
         ☐ B stripe
         ☐ C strike
         ☐ D strap

17 This meat stinks. It is not ☐ A sound   to eat
         ☐ B well
         ☐ C fit
         ☐ D proper

18 It is very easy for cars to skid on wet roads after a dry ☐ A spell
         ☐ B time
         ☐ C weather
         ☐ D while

19 You can't just do what you like. You must follow
the proper ☐ A processes
      ☐ B protocols
      ☐ C processions
      ☐ D procedures

20 To what do you ☐ A prescribe   your long life, old man?
      ☐ B attribute
      ☐ C explain
      ☐ D account

21 Sometimes it's better not to be noticed, so my advice to you is not to
stick your ☐ A neck   out
      ☐ B finger
      ☐ C nose
      ☐ D arm

22 Thanks for the invitation, but it's not my kind of party, so I think I'll
give it ☐ A a second thought   if you don't mind
    ☐ B the cold shoulder
    ☐ C a miss
    ☐ D a pass

23 I'm sorry I cannot stay long. This is just a ☐ A rush hour
    ☐ B flash in the pan
    ☐ C straw in the wind
    ☐ D flying visit

24 It's time to be frank with each other and put
    ☐ A the cat among the pigeons
    ☐ B our cards on the table
    ☐ C the cart before the horse
    ☐ D our shoulder to the wheel

25 He hadn't prepared a speech, he just made a few remarks
    ☐ A out of the back of his neck
    ☐ B up his sleeve
    ☐ C at first sight
    ☐ D off the cuff

C *Word building*

Choose the ending which forms a noun related to the word given. Only one ending is correct.

EXAMPLE: explain
    ☐ A expla- -inment
    ☐ B expla- -nation
    ☐ C expla- -inure
    ☐ D expla- -nity

The answer is B: 'explanation'.

26 Choose the ending which forms a noun related to the word 'arouse'.

☐ A arous-   -ement

☐ B arous-   -ure

☐ C arous-   -al

☐ D arous-   -ination

27 Choose the ending which forms a noun related to the word 'consume'.

☐ A consum-   -ption

☐ B consum-   -mation

☐ C consum-   -ality

☐ D consum-   -eness

28 Three of these words make their opposite by adding the prefix im-, e.g., mutable → immutable. Find the one that does not.

☐ A practical   ☐ B professional   ☐ C partial   ☐ D personal

29 Only one of these words can be changed to another by changing -ful to -less, e.g., hopeful to hopeless. Which one is it?

☐ A playful   ☐ B wrongful   ☐ C mournful   ☐ D pitiful

30 Three of these words make their opposite by adding the prefix dis-, e.g., reputable → disreputable. Find the one that does not.

☐ A obey   ☐ B please   ☐ C tolerate   ☐ D satisfy

D *Reading comprehension*

Fill in the gaps in the passage with the words which make sense.

EXAMPLE:

If you have broken both your legs, [1] _____ on a skiing holiday. After all, [2] _____ much fun just watching others enjoying themselves on the ski slopes.

[1] ☐ A everyone enjoys going

☐ B what a good idea it would be to go

☐ C why don't you go

☐ D there's not much point in going

The answer is D: 'there's not much point in going'.

[2] ☐ A what would be

☐ B you wouldn't have

☐ C you could have

☐ D there would be

The answer is B: 'you wouldn't have'.

The young married ladies of the village appreciated Fred when he came round each week to collect the insurance premiums. They looked [31] _____ chat, or simply a break from the boring routines of housework. But Hadley is a small village, and the tongues began to wag. The sight of Fred's old bike propped up against Mrs Fletcher's front wall or against the side of Mrs Turner's house for an hour or more, when everyone knew he [32] _____ two minutes, started the gossip among the older village women. The worst of these gossips was undoubtedly old Mrs Somersham. Her husband was not only the Manager of the local bank, [33] _____ Chairman of the Parish Council. She told him about her suspicions, but in that indirect way that makes gossip seem more [34] _____ the welfare of others. Mr Somersham took no notice at first, but then began to wonder. He heard one or two comments from other sources and [35] _____ believe the scandalous stories about Fred. He thought for a while, and decided to have a quiet word with one of the husbands.

31 ☐ A for someone to

☐ B as if they wanted a nice

☐ C forward to a friendly

☐ D after Fred and his

32 ☐ A had already been there

☐ B had to go every

☐ C always came back within

☐ D only needed to be there

33 ☐ A and even

☐ B or else

☐ C the so-called

☐ D but also

34 ☐ A   like genuine concern for

☐ B   than anything else

☐ C   a matter of friendship to

☐ D   dangerous than ever to

35 ☐ A   clearly refused to

☐ B   eventually began to

☐ C   couldn't bring himself to

☐ D   soon made everyone

E *Phonology*

> *In three of the four words, the underlined part is pronounced in the same way.*
> *Find the other word, in which the underlined part is pronounced differently.*
>
> EXAMPLE: ☐ A le<u>ar</u>n   ☐ B b<u>ir</u>d   ☐ C h<u>ear</u>t   ☐ D w<u>or</u>th
>
> *The answer is* C: 'heart'.

36 ☐ A disg<u>ui</u>se   ☐ B br<u>ui</u>se   ☐ C cr<u>ui</u>se   ☐ D s<u>ui</u>t

37 ☐ A <u>h</u>onourable   ☐ B <u>h</u>onesty   ☐ C <u>h</u>istoric   ☐ D <u>h</u>eir

38 ☐ A cr<u>ea</u>ture   ☐ B cr<u>ea</u>tive   ☐ C cr<u>ea</u>my   ☐ D cr<u>ea</u>se

39 Where does the stress fall in the word 'prejudicial'?

☐ A   ☐ B   ☐ C   ☐ D   ☐ E
pre   ju   dic   i   al

40 Three of these words can be pronounced in two different ways with a
change of meaning, e.g., the verb 'to graduate' [gradu-eit], and the noun
'a graduate' [gradu -ɛt]. Find the other word, which can be pronounced
in only one way.

☐ A estimate   ☐ B precipitate   ☐ C alternate   ☐ D delicate

LEVEL TWO

TEST 1

A *Grammar*

Choose the correct answer. Only one answer is correct.

EXAMPLE: Hurry up! The train ☐ A was   here shortly

                               ☐ B has been

                               ☐ C is

                               ☐ D will be

The correct answer is D: 'will be'.

1 She looked as if she ☐ A had seen   a ghost

                     ☐ B saw

                     ☐ C would see

                     ☐ D would have seen

2 Aren't you glad you came to the theatre with us?

Not really, I ☐ A rather preferred   to stay at home

               ☐ B would have preferred

               ☐ C had preferred

               ☐ D would prefer

3 The breakdown was said ☐ A to be caused by   a defective

                       ☐ B it was caused by   transformer

                       ☐ C that the cause was

                       ☐ D to have been caused by

4 Which sentence is closest in meaning to the sentence underlined?
Every morning my mother would feed the pigeons

    ☐ A Every morning my mother preferred to feed the pigeons herself

    ☐ B Every morning my mother insisted on feeding the pigeons

    ☐ C Every morning my mother wanted to feed the pigeons

    ☐ D Every morning my mother was in the habit of feeding the pigeons

5 She looks very frail, but

- ☐ A she's however quite strong, though
- ☐ B though she's quite strong
- ☐ C she's quite strong
- ☐ D however she's quite strong

6 Three of these verbs have the same form for infinitive, past tense and past participle, i.e., they are like put – put – put. Which one does not?

☐ A quit   ☐ B slit   ☐ C split   ☐ D sit

7 He denied

- ☐ A of   ever having been in Wandsworth
- ☐ B from
- ☐ C –
- ☐ D on

8 Don't worry about George. I will vouch

- ☐ A for   his complete honesty
- ☐ B of
- ☐ C with
- ☐ D to

9 The favourite was

- ☐ A on   the lead from the start and won the race easily
- ☐ B in
- ☐ C at
- ☐ D before

10 Are marsupials peculiar

- ☐ A from   Australia, or are they found elsewhere?
- ☐ B to
- ☐ C for
- ☐ D of

11 We expected him to be surprised, but in fact he didn't

- ☐ A shut   an eyelid
- ☐ B close
- ☐ C wink
- ☐ D bat

12 John is a very shrewd businessman: he never ☐ A fails   a trick

         ☐ B loses

         ☐ C misses

         ☐ D drops

13 It's dangerous to ☐ A let   off fireworks in the street

         ☐ B fire

         ☐ C bring

         ☐ D bang

14 When money is short, you just have to cut ☐ A down on   luxuries

         ☐ B out of

         ☐ C away from

         ☐ D up with

15 Are you going to put ☐ A up with   the boss's job when she retires?

         ☐ B in for

         ☐ C out to

         ☐ D in on

B *Vocabulary*

Choose the correct answer. Only one answer is correct.

EXAMPLE: How long did it ☐ A take   you to knit that scarf?

         ☐ B need

         ☐ C bring

         ☐ D make

The correct answer is A: 'take'.

16 On a cold winter's evening, there's nothing nicer than to sit in front of a

☐ A sparkling   fire

☐ B roaring

☐ C burning

☐ D glittering

17 The English are supposed to believe in ☐ A fair   play
                                                  ☐ B just
                                                  ☐ C square
                                                  ☐ D honest

18 You might miss your car if you sold it, but you'd be better off without it in the long ☐ A time
                        ☐ B view
                        ☐ C run
                        ☐ D reach

19 To the best of my ☐ A retention   , he married an Irish girl
                           ☐ B recall
                           ☐ C memory
                           ☐ D recollection

20 This pass will ☐ A determine   you to go anywhere
                     ☐ B enable
                     ☐ C accept
                     ☐ D approve

21 He just managed to survive by the skin of his ☐ A ears
                                           ☐ B nose
                                           ☐ C teeth
                                           ☐ D tongue

22 We have been very patient with our daughter and her inconsiderate behaviour, but the other night she didn't come back until four in the morning.

That really was the last ☐ A twig
                         ☐ B stick
                         ☐ C straw
                         ☐ D branch

23 Is it far to Stamford?

Not at all. It's only a ☐ A stone's throw   from here

                 ☐ B bird's eye view

                 ☐ C short cut

                 ☐ D step in the right direction

24 At first he seemed very keen to get married, but I think he's

beginning to ☐ A keep a stiff upper lip

            ☐ B have an axe to grind

            ☐ C hold tight

            ☐ D get cold feet

25 He thinks he's a failure so he drinks. The more he drinks, the more he

fails. It's a ☐ A roundabout

        ☐ B vicious circle

        ☐ C merry-go-round

        ☐ D wheel of fortune

C *Word building*

Choose the ending which forms a noun related to the word given. Only one ending is correct.

EXAMPLE: explain

       ☐ A expla-   -inment

       ☐ B expla-   -nation

       ☐ C expla-   -inure

       ☐ D expla-   -nity

The answer is B: 'explanation'.

26 Choose the ending which forms a noun related to the word 'conspicuous'.

     ☐ A conspicu-   -ousness

     ☐ B conspicu-   -ity

     ☐ C conspicu-   -ition

     ☐ D conspicu-   -osity

27 Choose the ending which forms a noun related to the word 'fluent'.

- [ ] A fluen- -ce
- [ ] B fluen- -tness
- [ ] C fluen- -cy
- [ ] D fluen- -tial

28 Three of these words make their opposite by adding the prefix im-, e.g., mutable → immutable. Find the one that does not.

- [ ] A persistent [ ] B measurable [ ] C possible [ ] D precise

29 Only one of these words can be changed to another by changing -less to -ful, e.g., hopeless to hopeful. Which one is it?

- [ ] A sleepless [ ] B homeless [ ] C regardless [ ] D harmless

30 Three of these words make their opposite by adding the prefix dis-, e.g., reputable → disreputable. Find the one that does not.

- [ ] A courage [ ] B amaze [ ] C advantage [ ] D courteous

D *Reading comprehension*

Fill in the gaps in the passage with the words which make sense.

EXAMPLE:

If you have broken both your legs, [1] _____ on a skiing holiday.
After all, [2] _____ much fun just watching others enjoying
themselves on the ski slopes.

[1] [ ] A everyone enjoys going

[ ] B what a good idea it would be to go

[ ] C why don't you go

[ ] D there's not much point in going

The answer is D: 'there's not much point in going'.

[2] [ ] A what would be

[ ] B you wouldn't have

[ ] C you could have

[ ] D there would be

The answer is B: 'you wouldn't have'.

Barcelona is not one of the most beautiful cities in the world: it is a busy, noisy, money-making city. All the same, on a warm spring morning, there are some fine places [31] _____ or two. The Rambles, a tree-lined avenue as broad and as beautiful as any Paris boulevard, is magical [32] _____, a colourful symphony of flowers and sunlight and people. Andrew was attending an international conference in Barcelona. It was the first time he had been to the city. Like most people, he [33] _____ about the Rambles, and was eager to go there. So he studied the conference programme and [34] _____ old Professor Thimble's lecture the next morning. I should perhaps explain that, when he was a young man, Thimble developed a theory about a possible relationship between the Basque language and certain Red Indian dialects; he [35] _____ lecture on the same subject ever since.

31 ☐ A in the old quarter of the city
   ☐ B whenever you go there for a holiday
   ☐ C to spend a quiet hour
   ☐ D listed in the best guide books

32 ☐ A at that time of day
   ☐ B for that matter
   ☐ C as far as spring is concerned
   ☐ D where you can spend the morning

33 ☐ A could hardly restrain himself
   ☐ B knew the reputation
   ☐ C was really interested
   ☐ D had heard a lot

34 ☐ A realised his colleagues were at
   ☐ B told himself he didn't want to hear
   ☐ C decided to spend the time reading
   ☐ D knew that he had already missed

35 ☐ A gave an identical
   ☐ B will probably give a boring
   ☐ C always attends another
   ☐ D has been giving the same

E *Phonology*

> *In three of the four words, the underlined part is pronounced in the same way. Find the other word, in which the underlined part is pronounced differently.*
>
> EXAMPLE: ☐ A le<u>ar</u>n ☐ B b<u>ir</u>d ☐ C h<u>ea</u>rt ☐ D w<u>or</u>th
>
> *The answer is* C: 'heart'.

36 ☐ A pol<u>i</u>ce ☐ B s<u>ei</u>ze ☐ C mach<u>i</u>ne ☐ D v<u>ei</u>l

37 ☐ A a<u>sc</u>ent ☐ B para<u>ch</u>ute ☐ C mi<u>ss</u>ion ☐ D vi<u>ci</u>ous

38 ☐ A p<u>e</u>nalty ☐ B sc<u>e</u>nic ☐ C epid<u>e</u>mic ☐ D l<u>e</u>vel

39 Where does the stress fall in the word 'extraordinary'?

☐ A   ☐ B   ☐ C ☐ D   ☐ E
extra   ord   in   a   ry

40 Three of these words can be pronounced in two different ways with a change of meaning, e.g., the verb 'to graduate' [gradu-eit], and the noun 'a graduate' [gradu -ɛt]. Find the other word, which can be pronounced in only one way.

☐ A associate ☐ B moderate ☐ C originate ☐ D appropriate

LEVEL TWO

TEST 2

A *Grammar*

> *Choose the correct answer. Only one answer is correct.*
>
> EXAMPLE: Hurry up! The train ☐ A was   here shortly
> ☐ B has been
> ☐ C is
> ☐ D will be
>
> *The correct answer is* D: 'will be'.

1 It looks as if he ☐ A shall miss   his train
☐ B had missed
☐ C would miss
☐ D has missed

2 Was she very disappointed?

Yes, she ☐ A liked to come   with you
☐ B would like to have come
☐ C liked to have come
☐ D would like to come

3 His death was attributed ☐ A to his having been bitten   by a snake
☐ B that he was bitten
☐ C to being bitten
☐ D that he had bitten

4 Which sentence is closest in meaning to the sentence underlined?
Should you see Eric, tell him I haven't forgotten my promise

☐ A You must see Eric and tell him I haven't forgotten my promise

☐ B You really ought to see Eric and tell him I haven't forgotten my promise

☐ C If you see Eric, tell him I haven't forgotten my promise

☐ D If you'd seen Eric, you could have told him I hadn't forgotten my promise

5 ☐ A How hard   you try, you can never get them all right

☐ B However hard

☐ C For as hard as

☐ D So hard as

6 Three of these verbs have the same form for past tense and past participle, like sit – sat – sat. Which one is different?

☐ A creep ☐ B peep ☐ C weep ☐ D sleep

7 Scientists cannot account ☐ A with   the disappearance of the dinosaurs

☐ B on

☐ C for

☐ D about

8 Nowadays the red squirrel is mainly confined ☐ A by Scots pine woods

☐ B in

☐ C at

☐ D to

9 Books and magazines should be exempt ☐ A from Value Added Tax

☐ B for

☐ C of

☐ D to

10 My dog is allergic ☐ A for   postmen

☐ B from

☐ C against

☐ D to

11 Everyone else will be wearing school uniform. You'll

- ☐ A stand up   like a sore thumb in that red dress
- ☐ B stick out
- ☐ C show off
- ☐ D catch on

12 I

- ☐ A bent   over backwards to help her, and she didn't even say
- ☐ B fell   thank you
- ☐ C stood
- ☐ D went

13 It seems a shame that so many animal species are

- ☐ A fading   out
- ☐ B passing
- ☐ C dying
- ☐ D wiping

14 You should get

- ☐ A down to   some revision: the exams are only a week away
- ☐ B up to
- ☐ C on to
- ☐ D away with

15 Where's her husband?

Didn't you hear? He has left her. He walked

- ☐ A off with   her a week ago
- ☐ B away from
- ☐ C out on
- ☐ D up to

B Vocabulary

Choose the correct answer. Only one answer is correct.

EXAMPLE: How long did it

- ☐ A take   you to knit that scarf?
- ☐ B need
- ☐ C bring
- ☐ D make

The correct answer is A: 'take'.

16 There's nothing as cosy on a cold evening as the warm

- [ ] A glare   of a fire
- [ ] B sparkle
- [ ] C glow
- [ ] D flame

17 The robbery took place in

- [ ] A bare   daylight
- [ ] B strong
- [ ] C open
- [ ] D broad

18 Is your house easy to find?

Well, it's a bit off the beaten

- [ ] A way   , I'm afraid
- [ ] B road
- [ ] C lane
- [ ] D track

19 I strongly resent the implication that I am lying.

Please

- [ ] A recall   your last statement
- [ ] B withdraw
- [ ] C remove
- [ ] D forswear

20 My mother

- [ ] A warned   me not to speak to strange men
- [ ] B prevented
- [ ] C foretold
- [ ] D deterred

21 I feel terrible. I didn't sleep

- [ ] A an eye   last night
- [ ] B a wink
- [ ] C a jot
- [ ] D an inch

22 You've had a ☐ A near   escape. I thought you'd never get away
            ☐ B narrow from him

            ☐ C short

            ☐ D close

23 You ought to buy his car off him: at one hundred pounds,

  it's real ☐ A money for old rope

         ☐ B cash in the bank

         ☐ C value for money

         ☐ D pennies from heaven

24 She seems to be angry with the whole world. She's got

  a chip ☐ A on her shoulder

        ☐ B in her bonnet

        ☐ C under her hat

        ☐ D between the ears

25 Father left us all a little bit of money in his will, but the

  ☐ A vested interest   of his estate went to Mother

  ☐ B square deal

  ☐ C pride and joy

  ☐ D lion's share

C *Word building*

Choose the ending which forms a noun related to the word given. Only one ending is correct.

EXAMPLE: explain

       ☐ A expla- –inment

       ☐ B expla- –nation

       ☐ C expla- –inure

       ☐ D expla- –nity

The answer is B: 'explanation'.

26 Choose the ending which forms a noun related to the word 'presume'.

☐ A presum-   -mation

☐ B presum-   -ption

☐ C presum-   -ity

☐ D presum-   -ativeness

27 Choose the ending which forms a noun related to the word 'false'.

☐ A fals-   -iness

☐ B fals-   -iety

☐ C fals-   -ehood

☐ D fals-   -icity

28 Three of these words make their opposite by adding the prefix im-, e.g., mutable → immutable. Find the one that does not.

☐ A maternal   ☐ B material   ☐ C proper   ☐ D potent

29 Only one of these words can be changed to another by changing -less to -ful, e.g., hopeless to hopeful. Which one is it?

☐ A pointless   ☐ B breathless   ☐ C penniless   ☐ D helpless

30 Three of these words make their opposite by adding the prefix dis-, e.g., reputable → disreputable. Find the one that does not.

☐ A honest   ☐ B perfect   ☐ C content   ☐ D obedient

D *Reading comprehension*

Fill in the gaps in the passage with the words which make sense.

EXAMPLE:

If you have broken both your legs, [1] ——— on a skiing holiday.
After all, [2] ——— much fun just watching others enjoying
themselves on the ski slopes.

[1] ☐ A everyone enjoys going

   ☐ B what a good idea it would be to go

   ☐ C why don't you go

   ☐ D there's not much point in going

The answer is D: 'there's not much point in going'.

[2] ☐ A what would be

☐ B you wouldn't have

☐ C you could have

☐ D there would be

The answer is B: 'you wouldn't have'.

Andrew was confined to a wheelchair, the result of an accident on the rugby field when he was at school. What he needed was someone to go with him to the Rambles. That evening, at dinner, he sat next to Tony Willingham, a man he [31] _____ once or twice before. It turned out that Tony knew Barcelona very well. Andrew decided to try his luck. He brought the conversation [32] _____ Professor Thimble and his theories. 'Thimble's done a lot of work on Basque, I'll admit,' said Tony, 'but, between you and me, I don't think he has anything new to say. I think I might give his lecture a miss. [33] _____ a stuffy lecture hall when the sun is shining.' 'Right! Why don't we sneak off and do some sightseeing?' Andrew suggested. 'What a good idea,' Tony said, but [34] _____ what it would mean to have to take someone round in a wheelchair. He felt guilty, but, all the same, it wouldn't be much fun for him, pushing a wheelchair around, getting the damned thing in and out of taxis, lifting it up and down steps, and so on. He despised [35] _____ selfish, but couldn't help the way he felt.

31 ☐ A hardly ever seen

☐ B had met

☐ C often used to meet

☐ D hadn't really met

32 ☐ A round to the subject of

☐ B which he had just had about

☐ C up to

☐ D in casually to discuss

33 ☐ A There's nothing to do with

☐ B What a terrible day to be in

☐ C It's a crime to stay in

☐ D How do you fancy getting away from

34 ☐ A he failed to reflect

☐ B he didn't like to mention

☐ C his heart sank as he realised

☐ D his mood improved when he thought

35 ☐ A the fact that he wasn't being

☐ B Andrew for making himself

☐ C the way he could never be so

☐ D himself for being so

E *Phonology*

> *In three of the four words, the underlined part is pronounced in the same way.*
> *Find the other word, in which the underlined part is pronounced differently.*
>
> EXAMPLE: ☐ A le<u>ar</u>n ☐ B b<u>ir</u>d ☐ C h<u>ear</u>t ☐ D w<u>or</u>th
>
> *The answer is* C: 'heart'.

36 ☐ A br<u>ea</u>ther ☐ B f<u>ea</u>ther ☐ C h<u>ea</u>ther ☐ D l<u>ea</u>ther

37 ☐ A a<u>ch</u>e ☐ B or<u>ch</u>estra ☐ C <u>ch</u>arity ☐ D <u>ch</u>orus

38 ☐ A purs<u>ui</u>t ☐ B s<u>ui</u>table ☐ C recr<u>ui</u>t ☐ D g<u>ui</u>lty

39 Where does the stress fall in the word 'characteristic'?

☐ A ☐ B ☐ C ☐ D ☐ E
char act er ist ic

40 Three of these words can be pronounced in two different ways with a
change of meaning, e.g., the verb 'to graduate' [gradu-eit], and the noun
'a graduate' [gradu -ɛt]. Find the other word, which can be pronounced
in only one way.

☐ A elaborate ☐ B concentrate ☐ C approximate

☐ D delegate

LEVEL TWO

TEST 3

A *Grammar*

Choose the correct answer. Only one answer is correct.

EXAMPLE: Hurry up! The train ☐ A was   here shortly

         ☐ B has been

         ☐ C is

         ☐ D will be

The correct answer is D: 'will be'.

---

1 It was as if the whole town ☐ A fell   asleep

         ☐ B had fallen

         ☐ C would have fallen

         ☐ D should fall

2 Do you mind staying behind to look after things?

No, but I ☐ A had loved to come   shopping with you instead

         ☐ B love coming

         ☐ C loved to have come

         ☐ D should love to have come

3 On ☐ A telling   he had won, he jumped for joy

         ☐ B he was told

         ☐ C being told

         ☐ D having told

4 Which sentence is closest in meaning to the sentence underlined?
<u>Will you be spending Christmas with the family?</u>

   ☐ A Do you intend to spend Christmas with the family?

   ☐ B May we invite you to spend Christmas with the family?

   ☐ C You don't really want to spend Christmas with the family, do you?

   ☐ D Why do you want to spend Christmas with the family?

5 You'll be all right ☐ A as soon   you've had something to eat

☐ B once

☐ C the time

☐ D so long

6 Three of these verbs have the same form for infinitive, past tense and past participle, i.e., they are like put – put – put. Which one does change?

☐ A shut ☐ B rid ☐ C spit ☐ D hit

7 It suddenly dawned ☐ A in   me where I had seen her before

☐ B to

☐ C over

☐ D on

8 Whenever there is a family row, my father always sides

☐ A by   my brother

☐ B to

☐ C along

☐ D with

9 Television has had a big impact ☐ A on   all our lives

☐ B for

☐ C in

☐ D over

10 ☐ A Through   virtue of his great age, he was allowed to have his own cell

☐ B By

☐ C In

☐ D For

11 If you ☐ A play   your cards right, you may get invited to the wedding

☐ B hold

☐ C call

☐ D deal

12 Joanna's taking three university degrees together. I know she's clever,

but I think she's bitten off more than she can ☐ A take   this time

☐ B eat

☐ C swallow

☐ D chew

13 Don't worry about the time. Just ☐ A pass   on till you've done your

☐ B put   work

☐ C pull

☐ D press

14 I want to be rich so I've decided to go ☐ A through with   accountancy

☐ B up on

☐ C in for

☐ D down to

15 Everybody in my class except me has gone ☐ A in for   measles

☐ B down with

☐ C on at

☐ D off to

B *Vocabulary*

Choose the correct answer. Only one answer is correct.

EXAMPLE: How long did it ☐ A take   you to knit that scarf?

☐ B need

☐ C bring

☐ D make

The correct answer is A: 'take'.

16 I managed to catch a ☐ A glimpse   of his wife as she got out of the car

☐ B glance

☐ C peep

☐ D sight

17 It was very ☐ A enterprising of you to start your own business
☐ B undertaking
☐ C initiative
☐ D incentive

18 To obtain stamps, put a 50p coin in the ☐ A slit and pull the knob
☐ B gap
☐ C slot
☐ D hole

19 How could you have spoken to my wife like that?
I'm sorry. I ☐ A vow I didn't know she was your wife
☐ B swear
☐ C testify
☐ D pledge

20 Food which has been condemned by the Ministry as dangerous to health
is still being sold by some ☐ A decadent traders
☐ B scrupulous
☐ C depraved
☐ D unscrupulous

21 Harry is completely unsuited for his job. He's what you might
call ☐ A a triangular peg in a round hole
☐ B an oval
☐ C a square
☐ D a badly shaped

22 I'll do my ☐ A true best to help you
☐ B full
☐ C honest
☐ D level

23 It's a complete misunderstanding. She really has got

hold of ☐ A the wrong end of the stick

☐ B the very idea

☐ C a bee in her bonnet

☐ D an axe to grind

24 He was so charming that he swept her ☐ A under the carpet in no

☐ B off her feet time

☐ C into his clutches

☐ D over the moon

25 I don't know whether he is guilty or not. Perhaps we should give him

the ☐ A benefit of the doubt this time

☐ B time of his life

☐ C thin end of the wedge

☐ D long and short of it

C *Word building*

Choose the ending which forms a noun related to the word given. Only one ending is correct.

EXAMPLE: explain

☐ A expla– –inment

☐ B expla– –nation

☐ C expla– –inure

☐ D expla– –nity

The answer is B: 'explanation'.

26 Choose the ending which forms a noun related to the word 'deny'.

☐ A den– –iance

☐ B den– –iment

☐ C den– –ial

☐ D den– –tition

27 Choose the ending which forms a noun related to the word 'anonymous'.

☐ A anonym- – –

☐ B anonym- –ity

☐ C anonym- –osity

☐ D anonym- –ousness

28 Three of these words make their opposite by adding the prefix im-, e.g., mutable → immutable. Find the one that does not.

☐ A mobile ☐ B penetrable ☐ C precise ☐ D majestic

29 Only one of these words can be changed to another by changing –less to –ful, e.g., hopeless to hopeful. Which one is it?

☐ A ruthless ☐ B mindless ☐ C featureless ☐ D priceless

30 Three of these words make their opposite by adding the prefix dis-, e.g., reputable → disreputable. Find the one that does not.

☐ A explain ☐ B loyal ☐ C organised ☐ D proportionate

D Reading comprehension

Fill in the gaps in the passage with the words which make sense.

EXAMPLE:

If you have broken both your legs, [1] _____ on a skiing holiday. After all, [2] _____ much fun just watching others enjoying themselves on the ski slopes.

[1] ☐ A everyone enjoys going

   ☐ B what a good idea it would be to go

   ☐ C why don't you go

   ☐ D there's not much point in going

The answer is D: 'there's not much point in going'.

[2] ☐ A what would be

   ☐ B you wouldn't have

   ☐ C you could have

   ☐ D there would be

The answer is B: 'you wouldn't have'.

Tony pushed Andrew in his wheelchair slowly down a pretty street by the side of the cathedral where the street musicians play. As they emerged from the street, a gypsy woman [31] _____ Tony a spray of heather, which is a sweet-scented herb that [32] _____ good luck. Tony [33] _____ he did not react. The woman then leant over the wheelchair and pinned the spray of heather to Andrew's lapel. Andrew smiled at her, wishing [34] _____ to say thank you. The woman smiled back at him, then turned back to Tony, begging, in that whining way that gypsies have, for a little money [35] _____ heather. Tony felt in his pocket and found that he had no change. 'You haven't got any change, have you, Andrew? We'd better give her a few pesetas or we'll never get rid of her.'

31 ☐ A turned down a side street and made
   ☐ B came up to them and offered
   ☐ C opened the door of the car and got
   ☐ D had just left in order to sell

32 ☐ A everyone knows about bringing
   ☐ B you will always have
   ☐ C is supposed to bring
   ☐ D was a moment of really

33 ☐ A was so startled that
   ☐ B looked as if
   ☐ C made an effort that
   ☐ D knew there was nothing for it but

34 ☐ A she would stop
   ☐ B there was no need for him
   ☐ C he knew the Spanish for
   ☐ D he had the words

35 ☐ A to buy a spray of
   ☐ B in return for the gift of
   ☐ C with which he paid for the
   ☐ D that he put in her hand for the

E *Phonology*

> In three of the four words, the underlined part is pronounced in the same way. Find the other word, in which the underlined part is pronounced differently.
>
> EXAMPLE: ☐ A l<u>ear</u>n ☐ B b<u>ir</u>d ☐ C h<u>ea</u>rt ☐ D w<u>or</u>th
>
> The answer is C: 'heart'.

36 ☐ A p<u>a</u>rade ☐ B ap<u>a</u>thetic ☐ C comp<u>a</u>nion ☐ D marm<u>a</u>lade

37 ☐ A re<u>s</u>earch ☐ B re<u>s</u>ent ☐ C re<u>s</u>emble ☐ D re<u>s</u>ist

38 ☐ A <u>i</u>tem ☐ B <u>i</u>diom ☐ C <u>i</u>dle ☐ D <u>i</u>deal

39 Where does the stress fall in the word 'superstitious'?

    ☐ A   ☐ B   ☐ C   ☐ D   ☐ E
    su   per   stit   i   ous

40 Three of these words can be pronounced in two different ways with a change of meaning, e.g., the verb 'to graduate' [gradu-eit], and the noun 'a graduate' [gradu -ɛt]. Find the other word, which can be pronounced in only one way.

    ☐ A separate ☐ B moderate ☐ C affectionate

    ☐ D discriminate

LEVEL THREE

TEST 1

A *Grammar*

Choose the correct answer. Only one answer is correct.

EXAMPLE: Hurry up! The train ☐ A was   here shortly

             ☐ B has been

             ☐ C is

             ☐ D will be

The correct answer is D: 'will be'.

1 ☐ A Had I known   earlier, I would have done it for you

   ☐ B If I knew

   ☐ C Did I know

   ☐ D By knowing

2 It was very kind of you to get me something for my birthday, but

you ☐ A didn't need buying   me such an expensive present

     ☐ B needn't buy

     ☐ C needn't have bought

     ☐ D hadn't needed to buy

3 The Minister is pleased to be able to announce that another 500 miles of

motorway ☐ A will be building   by the end of next year

     ☐ B are building

     ☐ C have been built

     ☐ D will have been built

4 Which sentence is closest in meaning to the sentence underlined?
<u>You needn't have bought me an expensive birthday present</u>

- [ ] A There was no need to buy me an expensive birthday present, but you did
- [ ] B There was no need to buy me an expensive birthday present, so it is just as well that you didn't
- [ ] C Why didn't you buy me an expensive birthday present?
- [ ] D I'm glad you didn't buy me an expensive birthday present

5 His life style was [ ] A so much   that everyone knew he was rich
[ ] B such
[ ] C so
[ ] D like

6 Three of these verbs have different forms for past tense and past participle, like speak – spoke – spoken. Which one does not?

[ ] A tread [ ] B weave [ ] C breed [ ] D freeze

7 Do you recall [ ] A of   the time we fell in the river with all our clothes on?
[ ] B –
[ ] C on
[ ] D to

8 If you join a club, you have to abide [ ] A by   its rules
[ ] B to
[ ] C –
[ ] D with

9 We managed to get to the airport with only a few minutes
- [ ] A for   spare
- [ ] B of
- [ ] C to
- [ ] D –

10 Tall people are more prone [ ] A on   backache than short people
[ ] B for
[ ] C in
[ ] D to

11 All I did was ask her how much she paid for her fur coat, and she nearly

- [ ] A blew   my head off
- [ ] B bit
- [ ] C broke
- [ ] D bent

12 I was so astonished that you could have

- [ ] A knocked   me down with a feather
- [ ] B swept
- [ ] C thrown
- [ ] D blown

13 Some of your comments are a bit strong: you should tone them

- [ ] A up   a bit
- [ ] B over
- [ ] C down
- [ ] D back

14 George has come

- [ ] A out on   a brilliant idea for losing weight
- [ ] B through for
- [ ] C across to
- [ ] D up with

15 Following the crime in Bridport High Street last Saturday afternoon, the police are checking

- [ ] A in for   anyone who was there at the time
- [ ] B up on
- [ ] C out of
- [ ] D over to

B *Vocabulary*

Choose the correct answer. Only one answer is correct.

EXAMPLE: How long did it

- [ ] A take   you to knit that scarf?
- [ ] B need
- [ ] C bring
- [ ] D make

The correct answer is A: 'take'.

16 He'll be back again ☐ A before long

☐ B within soon

☐ C after now

☐ D in a near time

17 This acid rain business sounds pretty bad, doesn't it?

It's only the ☐ A spit of the iceberg. There's worse to come

☐ B start

☐ C peak

☐ D tip

18 The dead woman was still ☐ A grabbing the flower in her hand

☐ B grasping

☐ C clutching

☐ D clenching

19 We were exhausted after ten hours of ☐ A strolling through deep snow

☐ B strutting

☐ C sauntering

☐ D trudging

20 He's a ☐ A plentiful author: he writes three books every year

☐ B prolific

☐ C abundant

☐ D generous

21 I'll never forgive Alan for breaking up the partnership.

You're barking up the wrong ☐ A street He had nothing to do with it

☐ B ship

☐ C chimney

☐ D tree

22 He's forever complaining about one thing or another. He's a

real ☐ A twist in the neck

☐ B ache

☐ C pain

☐ D itch

23 Frank is very good at doing simple accounts, but when it comes to
     auditing, he is completely ☐ A out of his depth

☐ B on the shelf

☐ C the worse for wear

☐ D under the weather

24 I know this part of Tuscany like the ☐ A back of my hand

☐ B skin of my teeth

☐ C hair on my head

☐ D nose on your face

25 That was the boss's husband you just insulted.
     You've really ☐ A kicked the bucket   this time

☐ B put your foot in it

☐ C gone to the dogs

☐ D made a mountain out of a molehill

C *Word building*

*Choose the ending which forms a noun related to the word given. Only one
ending is correct.*

EXAMPLE: explain

☐ A expla- -inment

☐ B expla- -nation

☐ C expla- -inure

☐ D expla- -nity

The answer is B: 'explanation'.

26 Choose the ending which forms a noun related to the word 'ridiculous'.

☐ A ridicul- -osity

☐ B ridicul- -ition

☐ C ridicul- -ement

☐ D ridicul- -e

27 Choose the ending which forms a noun related to the word 'rely'.

☐ A rel- -iament

☐ B rel- -ial

☐ C rel- -iance

☐ D rel- -iety

28 Three of these words make their opposite by adding the prefix ir-, e.g., religious → irreligious. Find the one that does not.

☐ A reconcilable   ☐ B replaceable   ☐ C retrievable

☐ D reasonable

29 Only one of these words can be changed to another by changing -less to -ful, e.g., hopeless to hopeful. Which one is it?

☐ A restless   ☐ B senseless   ☐ C lifeless   ☐ D speechless

30 Three of these words make their opposite by adding the prefix dis-, e.g., reputable → disreputable. Find the one that does not.

☐ A advantage   ☐ B confirm   ☐ C similar   ☐ D locate

D *Reading comprehension*

Fill in the gaps in the passage with the words which make sense.

EXAMPLE:

If you have broken both your legs, [1] _____ on a skiing holiday.
After all, [2] _____ much fun just watching others enjoying themselves on the ski slopes.

[1] ☐ A everyone enjoys going

☐ B what a good idea it would be to go

☐ C why don't you go

☐ D there's not much point in going

The answer is D: 'there's not much point in going'.

[2] ☐ A what would be

☐ B you wouldn't have

☐ C you could have

☐ D there would be

The answer is B: 'you wouldn't have'.

It was the day of Henry Ground's funeral. Relatives who had not spoken for years smiled at each other and promised to stay in touch. And, of course, everyone had a favourite story [31] _____ about Henry, the world's greatest practical joker.

'I was once having dinner with him in a posh restaurant,' said one. 'When the wine waiter brought the wine, he poured a drop into Henry's glass and waited with a superior expression on his face as if [32] _____ Henry could possibly know anything about wine. So, Henry dipped his thumb and forefinger into the wine in his glass, [33] _____ tasting it, the way any normal person would do. Then he put his hand to his ear and rolled his forefinger and thumb together as if he were *listening* to the quality of the wine! Then he nodded to the waiter solemnly, [34] _____ say, "Yes, that's fine. You may serve it." You should have seen the wine waiter's face! And how Henry managed to [35] _____ face, I'll never know!'

31 ☐ A that he was dying to tell
   ☐ B it was a good one
   ☐ C which nobody knew
   ☐ D for telling all

32 ☐ A to say that
   ☐ B it was a sure thing that
   ☐ C he did not believe that
   ☐ D there was no reason for

33 ☐ A by way of
   ☐ B while
   ☐ C there was no way of
   ☐ D instead of

34 ☐ A which they always
   ☐ B as if to
   ☐ C waiting to
   ☐ D to make him

35 ☐ A make a

    ☐ B hide his

    ☐ C keep a straight

    ☐ D look at the waiter face to

E *Phonology*

> *In three of the four words, the underlined part is pronounced in the same way. Find the other word, in which the underlined part is pronounced differently.*
>
> EXAMPLE: ☐ A l<u>ear</u>n ☐ B b<u>ir</u>d ☐ C h<u>ear</u>t ☐ D w<u>or</u>th
>
> *The answer is* C: 'heart'.

36 ☐ A compl<u>ai</u>n ☐ B barg<u>ai</u>n ☐ C ascert<u>ai</u>n ☐ D camp<u>aig</u>n

37 ☐ A bro<u>ch</u>ure ☐ B <u>s</u>ugar ☐ C s<u>ch</u>olarship ☐ D cons<u>ci</u>ous

38 ☐ A d<u>y</u>namic ☐ B h<u>y</u>pocrite ☐ C c<u>y</u>nicism ☐ D t<u>y</u>pical

39 Where does the stress fall in the word 'deliberately'?

    ☐ A   ☐ B   ☐ C   ☐ D   ☐ E
    de   lib   er   ate   ly

40 Three of these words can be pronounced in two different ways with a change of meaning, e.g., the verb 'to graduate' [gradu-eit], and the noun 'a graduate' [gradu -ɛt]. Find the other word, which can be pronounced in only one way.

    ☐ A wind ☐ B kind ☐ C tear ☐ D lead

LEVEL THREE

TEST 2

A *Grammar*

Choose the correct answer. Only one answer is correct.

EXAMPLE: Hurry up! The train ☐ A was   here shortly

                 ☐ B has been

                 ☐ C is

                 ☐ D will be

The correct answer is D: 'will be'.

---

1 ☐ A If you had seen   Mary, give her my love

   ☐ B Do you see

   ☐ C By seeing

   ☐ D Should you see

2 Joe's going away, isn't he?

   Maybe, but he ☐ A hasn't to go   for long because he hasn't taken a suitcase

               ☐ B mustn't go

               ☐ C can't go

               ☐ D can't be going

3 The Minister was pleased to be able to announce that another 500 miles

   of motorway ☐ A had been built   by the end of last year

             ☐ B have been building

             ☐ C are being built

             ☐ D were building

4 Which sentence is closest in meaning to the sentence underlined?
Bubu tribesmen, who live by the river, never learn to swim

☐ A Only the Bubus who live by the river know how to swim

☐ B The Bubus who can swim are the ones who live by the river

☐ C All Bubus live by the river but none of them can swim

☐ D Bubus only learn to swim if they live by the river

5 What are you going to do ☐ A once that the children have all left home?

☐ B now

☐ C in view

☐ D since

6 Three of these verbs have the same form for past tense and past participle, like sit – sat – sat. Which one is different?

☐ A deal ☐ B write ☐ C dwell ☐ D kneel

7 Dispose ☐ A – unwanted medicines by flushing them down the toilet

☐ B from

☐ C of

☐ D to

8 I had to plough ☐ A through forty reports before I found what I wanted

☐ B into

☐ C over

☐ D across

9 An Englishman really takes pride ☐ A in keeping his garden neat and tidy

☐ B on

☐ C for

☐ D to

10 Do you think we could meet sometime ☐ A through the weekend?

☐ B on

☐ C in

☐ D over

11 No use ☐ A blaming   over spilt milk. What's done is done

☐ B shouting

☐ C sitting

☐ D crying

12 Stop ☐ A hiding   about the bush: say what you really mean

☐ B running

☐ C beating

☐ D jumping

13 The topic of drugs seems to ☐ A crop   up whenever Joe joins the

☐ B bring   conversation

☐ C jump

☐ D toss

14 When are you going to mend that broken window?

Don't worry, I'll get ☐ A up to   it one of these days

☐ B over with

☐ C around to

☐ D down on

15 For all the latest pop music, tune ☐ A on at   your favourite radio

☐ B in to   station

☐ C up with

☐ D along for

B *Vocabulary*

Choose the correct answer. Only one answer is correct.

EXAMPLE: How long did it ☐ A take   you to knit that scarf?

☐ B need

☐ C bring

☐ D make

The correct answer is A: 'take'.

16 Don't trust him. He's ☐ A perfectly   dishonest
☐ B utterly
☐ C purely
☐ D exactly

17 You seem to be in very good ☐ A shape   .Do you do a lot of
exercise?
☐ B cut
☐ C order
☐ D build

18 At the start of a game, how do they decide who should go first?
They ☐ A pitch   a coin
☐ B cast
☐ C throw
☐ D toss

19 If you ask her what her name is, she usually says, 'T–T–T–Teresa
J-J-J-Jane'. The poor girl has a terrible ☐ A stumble
☐ B stagger
☐ C stutter
☐ D strangle

20 His name is Charles Norman Biggs, but he writes it as Charles
Norman-Biggs. Don't you think that is rather ☐ A precious   ?
☐ B artificial
☐ C presumed
☐ D pretentious

21 Why don't you draw out all your money and enjoy yourself, or are you
saving it for a ☐ A foggy   day?
☐ B rainy
☐ C windy
☐ D cloudy

22 He gets up every morning at the ☐ A glow   of dawn to milk the
                                    ☐ B light   cows
                                    ☐ C crack
                                    ☐ D split

23 Don't quote me. What I am about to tell you is off the ☐ A record
                                                          ☐ B shelf
                                                          ☐ C cuff
                                                          ☐ D book

24 Is John really going to join the Foreign Legion?

   Well, he said he was, but I think he ☐ A has half a mind   about it
                                        ☐ B has stopped short   now
                                        ☐ C has thought better
                                        ☐ D is in two minds

25 When the boss found out that I'd wiped out the entire database, he really

   ☐ A jumped in at the deep end   . I've never seen him so angry
   ☐ B took leave of his senses
   ☐ C stuck his neck out
   ☐ D hit the roof

C Word building

Choose the ending which forms a noun related to the word given. Only one
ending is correct.

EXAMPLE: explain

        ☐ A expla- -inment
        ☐ B expla- -nation
        ☐ C expla- -inure
        ☐ D expla- -nity

The answer is B: 'explanation'.

26 Choose the ending which forms a noun related to the word 'notorious'.

- ☐ A notori- -ety
- ☐ B notori- -osity
- ☐ C notori- -ability
- ☐ D notori- -liness

27 Choose the ending which forms a noun related to the word 'convince'.

- ☐ A conv- -iction
- ☐ B conv- -incement
- ☐ C conv- -ention
- ☐ D conv- -icture

28 Three of these words make their opposite by adding the prefix ir-, e.g., religious → irreligious. Find the one that does not.

☐ A reversible ☐ B redeemable ☐ C relevant ☐ D rebellious

29 Only one of these words can be changed to another by changing -less to -ful, e.g., hopeless to hopeful. Which one is it?

☐ A nameless ☐ B faithless ☐ C aimless ☐ D cloudless

30 Three of these words make their opposite by adding the prefix dis-, e.g., reputable → disreputable. Find the one that does not.

☐ A hearten ☐ B integrate ☐ C attend ☐ D prove

D *Reading comprehension*

Fill in the gaps in the passage with the words which make sense.

EXAMPLE:

If you have broken both your legs, [1] _____ on a skiing holiday.
After all, [2] _____ much fun just watching others enjoying
themselves on the ski slopes.

[1] ☐ A everyone enjoys going

   ☐ B what a good idea it would be to go

   ☐ C why don't you go

   ☐ D there's not much point in going

The answer is D: 'there's not much point in going'.

[2] ☐ A what would be

☐ B you wouldn't have

☐ C you could have

☐ D there would be

The answer is B: 'you wouldn't have'.

The lawyer began to read out Henry's will. 'Dear friends,' he began, 'I have set you a little competition. Each of you in turn must tell the funniest joke he or she can think of, and the one who provokes the most laughter will inherit my fortune. My lawyer will [31] _____ the best joke.' 'So, ladies and gentlemen,' said the lawyer, putting the will down on the table, 'it's up to you now. Who will go first? May I [32] _____ go in alphabetical order of surnames?' The first person stood up and told a very funny joke about an Englishman who fell in love with his umbrella. When he finished, he was in tears of laughter, [33] _____ his own jokes. The rest of the company remained absolutely silent. You could tell from their red faces and their screwed-up eyes that they found the joke funny, but [34] _____ laugh, and give him the chance to win the competition. The second told a story about a three-legged pig. When she sat down, the others coughed, pretended to sneeze, dropped pencils under the table – [35] _____ their laughter. And so it went on, joke after joke, the sort of jokes that make your sides ache. And nobody dared to laugh!

31 ☐ A enjoy listening to

☐ B have to decide

☐ C act as referee for

☐ D be the sole judge of

32 ☐ A ask whether you

☐ B remind you to

☐ C suggest that you

☐ D propose the first to

33 ☐ A for he always laughed at

☐ B although he was very fond of

☐ C in order to enjoy

☐ D as he wanted everyone to be amused by

34 ☐ A everyone started to

☐ B anybody who had the courage to

☐ C not one of them was prepared to

☐ D it wasn't funny enough to cause a

35 ☐ A trying to avoid

☐ B anything to cover up

☐ C everything which increased

☐ D all behind

E *Phonology*

> *In three of the four words, the underlined part is pronounced in the same way. Find the other word, in which the underlined part is pronounced differently.*
>
> EXAMPLE: ☐ A le<u>ar</u>n ☐ B b<u>ir</u>d ☐ C h<u>ea</u>rt ☐ D w<u>or</u>th
>
> *The answer is* C: 'heart'.

36 ☐ A h<u>e</u>roine ☐ B p<u>e</u>nalty ☐ C po<u>e</u>tic ☐ D conv<u>e</u>nient

37 ☐ A privile<u>ge</u> ☐ B colla<u>ge</u> ☐ C colle<u>ge</u> ☐ D messa<u>ge</u>

38 ☐ A h<u>ear</u>say ☐ B end<u>ear</u>ment ☐ C reh<u>ear</u>se ☐ D b<u>ear</u>d

39 Where does the stress fall in the word 'arithmetical'?

☐ A   ☐ B   ☐ C   ☐ D   ☐ E
ar   ith   met   ic   al

40 Three of these words can be pronounced in two different ways with a change of meaning, e.g., the verb 'to graduate' [gradu-eit], and the noun 'a graduate' [gradu -ɕt]. Find the other word, which can be pronounced in only one way.

☐ A house ☐ B confuse ☐ C use ☐ D excuse

LEVEL THREE

TEST 3

A *Grammar*

> *Choose the correct answer. Only one answer is correct.*
>
> EXAMPLE: Hurry up! The train ☐ A was   here shortly
> ☐ B has been
> ☐ C is
> ☐ D will be
>
> *The correct answer is* D: 'will be'.

1 Would you have married me if I had asked you?

Only if you ☐ A had promised   to stop flirting with other
☐ B have promised   men
☐ C would have promised
☐ D promised

2 Is swimming under water very difficult?

No, it's just a matter ☐ A to be able   to control your breathing
☐ B of being able
☐ C that you are able
☐ D being able

3 Dinosaurs are thought to ☐ A die out   millions of years ago
☐ B have died out
☐ C having died out
☐ D dying out

4 Which sentence is closest in meaning to the sentence underlined?
The Bubu tribesmen who live by the river are good swimmers

☐ A Good Bubu swimmers often live by the river

☐ B The Bubus who are good swimmers are the ones who live by the river

☐ C Bubus who live far from the river cannot learn to swim

☐ D All Bubus are good swimmers because they live by the river

5 ☐ A Much as I love you, I cannot let you have any more money

☐ B Whether

☐ C Also

☐ D However

6 Three of these verbs have the same form for past tense and past participle, like sit – sat – sat. Which one is different?

☐ A sing ☐ B fling ☐ C cling ☐ D string

7 Joe studied medicine and then then decided to specialise

☐ A to gynaecology

☐ B for

☐ C in

☐ D on

8 Mrs Gooby is a busybody: she loves prying ☐ A in other people's business

☐ B into

☐ C out

☐ D after

9 I'm not ☐ A with my best first thing in the morning

☐ B –

☐ C on

☐ D at

10 ☐ A Within no circumstances should you drink the tap water

☐ B On

☐ C By

☐ D Under

11 If he's in trouble, it's his own fault. I personally wouldn't

- [ ] A lift a finger to help him
- [ ] B turn
- [ ] C bend
- [ ] D raise

12 The rumours about a government crisis

- [ ] A caught like wildfire
- [ ] B went
- [ ] C spread
- [ ] D blew

13 The new sofa

- [ ] A blends in well with the rest of the furniture
- [ ] B combines
- [ ] C mixes
- [ ] D sets

14 Don't worry if she still plays with dolls: she'll soon grow

- [ ] A away from it
- [ ] B out of
- [ ] C up off
- [ ] D down on

15 All right! I forgive you. Please stop going

- [ ] A off with it!
- [ ] B up to
- [ ] C in with
- [ ] D on about

B *Vocabulary*

Choose the correct answer. Only one answer is correct.

EXAMPLE: How long did it ☐ A take   you to knit that scarf?

☐ B need

☐ C bring

☐ D make

The correct answer is A: 'take'.

16 I wouldn't even go out with a Martian, let ☐ A away   marry one

☐ B apart

☐ C aside

☐ D alone

17 He retired from the Army with the ☐ A rank   of Lieutenant
Colonel

☐ B standard

☐ C grade

☐ D class

18 You deserve a ☐ A pat   on the back for the good work you have
done

☐ B tap

☐ C clap

☐ D stroke

19 He hit his toe against a stone, which caused

him to ☐ A strangle   and fall to the ground

☐ B stumble

☐ C struggle

☐ D stammer

20 There were ☐ A cartoons   on all the walls advertising the
concert

☐ B insertions

☐ C posters

☐ D propaganda

21 We thought you'd lose your chance, but you made it

at the ☐ A eleventh hour

☐ B last

☐ C final

☐ D closing

22 Thousands came to pay their ☐ A regret at the President's

☐ B respects graveside

☐ C reverence

☐ D regards

23 I don't know how I'm going to find the money for the rent,

☐ A in view of going out and robbing a bank

☐ B up to

☐ C short of

☐ D otherwise

24 You won't be prosecuted after all, madam.

That's a ☐ A piece of my mind ! I was really worried

☐ B free for all

☐ C load off my mind

☐ D blessing in disguise

25 Just because we've had a good year, this does not mean that we cannot

do better: we must not ☐ A have our head in the clouds

☐ B bury our heads in the sand

☐ C count our blessings

☐ D rest on our laurels

C *Word building*

Choose the ending which forms a noun related to the word given. Only one ending is correct.

EXAMPLE: explain

☐ A expla- -inment

☐ B expla- -nation

☐ C expla- -inure

☐ D expla- -nity

The answer is B: 'explanation'.

26 Choose the ending which forms a noun related to the word 'obey'.

☐ A obe- -yance

☐ B obe- -iness

☐ C obe- -sity

☐ D obe- -dience

27 Choose the ending which forms a noun related to the word 'legal'.

☐ A lega- -lity

☐ B lega- -ncy

☐ C lega- -tion

☐ D lega- -lry

28 Three of these words make their opposite by adding the prefix ir-, e.g., religious → irreligious. Find the one that does not.

☐ A responsible ☐ B reliable ☐ C regular ☐ D rational

29 Only one of these words can be changed to another by changing -less to -ful, e.g., hopeless to hopeful. Which one is it?

☐ A odourless ☐ B reckless ☐ C meaningless ☐ D listless

30 Three of these words make their opposite by adding the prefix dis-, e.g., reputable → disreputable. Find the one that does not.

☐ A credit ☐ B taste ☐ C observe ☐ D belief

D *Reading comprehension*

Fill in the gaps in the passage with the words which make sense.

EXAMPLE:

If you have broken both your legs, [1] _____ on a skiing holiday.
After all, [2] _____ much fun just watching others enjoying
themselves on the ski slopes.

[1] ☐ A everyone enjoys going

  ☐ B what a good idea it would be to go

  ☐ C why don't you go

  ☐ D there's not much point in going

The answer is D: 'there's not much point in going'.

[2] ☐ A what would be

  ☐ B you wouldn't have

  ☐ C you could have

  ☐ D there would be

The answer is B: 'you wouldn't have'.

[31] _____ the last joke had been told, every one of the twelve people
attending the reading out of Henry's will was sitting perfectly still,
desperately holding in the laughter that was bursting to get out. The
suppressed laughter [32] _____ a pressure that it was like a volcano ready to
erupt. Silence. Painful silence. Suddenly, the lawyer sneezed. Then he took
out a large red spotted handkerchief and blew his nose. Bbbrrrrrrppp. That
was enough. Someone burst out laughing, [33] _____ to hold it in any
longer. That started the others off. [34] _____ they were all doubled up,
tears streaming from their eyes, their shoulders heaving with laughter. Of
course, they were not just laughing at the sneeze, nor even at the jokes. No,
they were laughing at themselves [35] _____ that Henry had led them into
his last, and funniest, practical joke, setting their need to laugh against their
greed for money.

31 ☐ A By the time
☐ B It was not until
☐ C For several minutes after
☐ D Nevertheless

32 ☐ A was so
☐ B had built up such
☐ C produced
☐ D caused everyone to feel

33 ☐ A unable
☐ B waiting till the last moment
☐ C hoping to be able
☐ D as there was no time

34 ☐ A Sooner or later,
☐ B As it happens,
☐ C In no time,
☐ D After all,

35 ☐ A although they could see at last
☐ B because there was no fear
☐ C while it was clear as daylight
☐ D as it dawned on each one of them

E *Phonology*

> *In three of the four words, the underlined part is pronounced in the same way.*
> *Find the other word, in which the underlined part is pronounced differently.*
>
> EXAMPLE: ☐ A l<u>ear</u>n ☐ B b<u>ir</u>d ☐ C h<u>ear</u>t ☐ D w<u>or</u>th
>
> *The answer is* C: 'heart'.

36 ☐ A f<u>ou</u>l ☐ B br<u>oo</u>ch ☐ C s<u>ou</u>l ☐ D f<u>oa</u>l

37 ☐ A c<u>o</u>lonel ☐ B j<u>ou</u>rnal ☐ C inf<u>er</u>nal ☐ D m<u>our</u>nful

38 ☐ A taught   ☐ B laughter   ☐ C naughty   ☐ D slaughter

39 Where does the stress fall in the word 'ostentatiously'?

☐ A   ☐ B   ☐ C   ☐ D   ☐ E
ost   ent   at   ious   ly

40 Three of these words can be pronounced in two different ways with a change of meaning, e.g., the verb 'to graduate' [gradu-eit], and the noun 'a graduate' [gradu -ɛt]. Find the other word, which can be pronounced in only one way.

☐ A sow   ☐ B row   ☐ C bow   ☐ D mow

REVIEW TEST

A *Grammar*

Choose the correct answer. Only one answer is correct.

EXAMPLE: Hurry up! The train ☐ A was   here shortly

☐ B has been

☐ C is

☐ D will be

The correct answer is D: 'will be'.

1 If I hadn't ☐ A had it done   by an expert, it wouldn't look so nice

☐ B done it

☐ C have it done

☐ D have done it

2 ☐ A I'd rather not   say anything more

☐ B I hadn't rather

☐ C I rather didn't

☐ D I'd rather not to

3 Mr Jones says you are all to ☐ A have given   an extra day off

☐ B being given

☐ C be given

☐ D give

4 Which sentence is closest in meaning to the sentence underlined?
My daughter has married a ninety-year-old man? <u>It doesn't bear
thinking about</u>

☐ A It's difficult to think about

☐ B I never thought of that

☐ C I don't want to think about it

☐ D Whatever made her decide to do that?

5 ☐ A Despite   popular opinion, many Welsh people do not speak
     ☐ B Against   Welsh
     ☐ C Contrary to
     ☐ D Opposite

6 Three of these verbs have the same form for past tense and past
    participle, like sit – sat – sat. Which one is different?

     ☐ A wring   ☐ B sting   ☐ C hang   ☐ D ring

7 Is it possible to be inoculated ☐ A for   the illness called love?
                                        ☐ B against
                                        ☐ C in
                                        ☐ D to

8 I should like to emphasize ☐ A on   the difference between hope and
                                   ☐ B for   wish
                                   ☐ C –
                                   ☐ D to

9 Can I please have a room ☐ A for   my own when I grow up?
                                 ☐ B by
                                 ☐ C to
                                 ☐ D of

10 Payment of this invoice should be made ☐ A within   thirty days
                                                ☐ B before
                                                ☐ C by
                                                ☐ D up to

11 They ☐ A show   lip service to the issue, but they won't do anything
              ☐ B make   about it
              ☐ C pay
              ☐ D do

12 Doctor, what's this lump on my head?

Let me ☐ A turn   your mind at rest. It's nothing serious

☐ B bring

☐ C make

☐ D set

13 Was I asleep? I must have ☐ A slipped   off

☐ B fallen

☐ C dipped

☐ D nodded

14 Please don't walk so quickly. I can hardly keep ☐ A next to   you

☐ B up with

☐ C aside of

☐ D along with

15 The strikers refused to accept management's offer, but decided instead

to stick ☐ A out for   better working conditions

☐ B on to

☐ C up with

☐ D back on

B *Vocabulary*

Choose the correct answer. Only one answer is correct.

EXAMPLE: How long did it ☐ A take   you to knit that scarf?

☐ B need

☐ C bring

☐ D make

The correct answer is A: 'take'.

16 The tap is ☐ A watering   .It probably needs a new washer

☐ B dripping

☐ C trickling

☐ D dropping

17 The guerrillas attacked the village. Nobody was left alive: they

☐ A assassinated every one of the inhabitants

☐ B slaughtered

☐ C decimated

☐ D disposed

18 She divorced him on the ☐ A grounds of cruelty

☐ B basis

☐ C reasons

☐ D causes

19 The play was badly under-rehearsed. Finally the audience started booing

and ☐ A sneering the players

☐ B sniggering

☐ C jeering

☐ D clapping

20 Parks, swimming pools and libraries are all examples

of public ☐ A conveniences

☐ B entertainments

☐ C provisions

☐ D amenities

21 There are a lot of crooked people in big cities. If you don't want to be

cheated, you'll need to keep your ☐ A mind about you

☐ B wits

☐ C head

☐ D brains

22 If you want to marry the boss's daughter, you'll just have to go in and

tell him straight: go on, be a man: take the bull by the ☐ A tail !

☐ B horns

☐ C teeth

☐ D hair

23 It was supposed to be a social occasion, but my wife and her

boss talked ☐ A shop   all through the meal

             ☐ B through their hats

             ☐ C off the cuff

             ☐ D in turns

24 How do you calculate the distance to the horizon?

As a ☐ A trick of the trade   , it's 7 miles + 1 mile per 100 ft above sea

      ☐ B golden rule   level

      ☐ C free hand

      ☐ D rule of thumb

25 Nobody's seen him since the day he got up and walked out. He just

vanished ☐ A behind the scenes

          ☐ B under the counter

          ☐ C into thin air

          ☐ D like a shot in the dark

C *Word building*

Choose the ending which forms a noun related to the word given. Only one ending is correct.

EXAMPLE: explain

        ☐ A expla- -inment

        ☐ B expla- -nation

        ☐ C expla- -inure

        ☐ D expla- -nity

The answer is B: 'explanation'.

26 Choose the ending which forms a noun related to the word 'revive'.

     ☐ A reviv- -acity

     ☐ B reviv- -ation

     ☐ C reviv- -al

     ☐ D reviv- -eliness

27 Choose the ending which forms a noun related to the word 'seize'.

☐ A seiz– –ement

☐ B seiz– –ure

☐ C seiz– –al

☐ D seiz– –e

28 Three of these words make their opposite by adding the prefix im-, e.g., mutable → immutable. Find the one that does not.

☐ A plausible ☐ B perceptible ☐ C palatable ☐ D passable

29 Only one of these words can be changed to another by changing -ful to -less, e.g., hopeful to hopeless. Which one is it?

☐ A stressful ☐ B woeful ☐ C fearful ☐ D eventful

30 Three of these words make their opposite by adding the prefix dis-, e.g., reputable → disreputable. Find the one that does not.

☐ A fire ☐ B appear ☐ C continue ☐ D allow

D *Reading comprehension*

In the following dialogues, which phrase or sentence means the same as the one underlined?

EXAMPLE: How would you like to join us for a swim?
<u>I'm all in!</u>

☐ A No thanks, I'm too tired.

☐ B Definitely!

☐ C I don't mind.

☐ D I've already had a swim.

The answer is A: 'No thanks, I'm too tired.'

31 Can I have a rise?
<u>Out of the question!</u>

☐ A Of course!

☐ B I don't understand exactly what you mean.

☐ C What a stupid thing to ask for!

☐ D Impossible!

32 Would you take the job if they offered it to you?
<u>You bet!</u>

☐ A There's a good chance that I would!

☐ B What is your opinion?

☐ C I'm not going to tell you!

☐ D Definitely!

33 I never take any notice of him!
<u>It's all right for you to talk.</u>

☐ A The situation is easier for you than it is for me.

☐ B You always know what's best.

☐ C I wish I knew what to say.

☐ D Don't worry. Nobody will hear you.

34 Surely John's not the kind of man to go around stealing things?
<u>I wouldn't put it past him.</u>

☐ A I believe that he wouldn't do such a thing.

☐ B I believe that he is too mature to do such a thing.

☐ C I believe that he is capable of doing such a thing.

☐ D I believe that he has often done such things in the past.

35 Look at this plant. Someone has broken the stem.
<u>Well I never!</u>

☐ A I didn't do it!

☐ B I can't believe it!

☐ C I'm sure it will recover!

☐ D It's nothing to do with me!

E *Phonology*

In three of the four words, the underlined part is pronounced in the same way. Find the other word, in which the underlined part is pronounced differently.

EXAMPLE: ☐ A l<u>ear</u>n   ☐ B b<u>ir</u>d   ☐ C h<u>ear</u>t   ☐ D w<u>or</u>th

The answer is C: 'heart'.

---

36 ☐ A surg<u>eo</u>n   ☐ B thor<u>ou</u>gh   ☐ C quest<u>io</u>ns   ☐ D t<u>ou</u>gh

37 ☐ A pract<u>ice</u>   ☐ B dev<u>ice</u>   ☐ C serv<u>ice</u>   ☐ D off<u>ice</u>

38 ☐ A t<u>i</u>tle   ☐ B dest<u>i</u>ny   ☐ C div<u>i</u>ne   ☐ D al<u>i</u>gn

39 Where does the stress fall in the word 'administrative'?

☐ A   ☐ B   ☐ C   ☐ D   ☐ E
  ad   min   ist   rat   ive

40 Three of these words can be pronounced in two different ways with a change of meaning, e.g., the verb 'to graduate' [gradu-eit], and the noun 'a graduate' [gradu -ɛt]. Find the other word, which can be pronounced in only one way.

☐ A wound   ☐ B live   ☐ C tow   ☐ D minute

KEY TO TESTS

No.	LEVEL ONE			LEVEL TWO			LEVEL THREE			Review Test
	Test 1	Test 2	Test 3	Test 1	Test 2	Test 3	Test 1	Test 2	Test 3	
1	C	C	C	A	D	B	A	D	A	A
2	A	A	A	B	B	D	C	D	B	A
3	D	B	D	D	A	C	D	A	B	C
4	B	B	C	D	C	A	A	C	B	C
5	B	D	B	C	B	B	B	B	A	C
6	C	B	C	D	B	C	C	B	A	D
7	D	A	A	C	C	D	B	C	C	B
8	B	D	A	A	D	D	A	A	B	C
9	B	C	D	B	A	A	C	A	D	D
10	A	B	B	B	D	B	D	D	D	A
11	C	B	C	D	B	A	B	D	A	C
12	A	A	D	C	A	D	A	C	C	D
13	C	D	B	A	C	D	C	A	A	D
14	D	C	A	A	A	C	D	C	B	B
15	A	D	B	B	C	B	B	B	D	A
16	C	C	B	B	C	A	A	B	D	B
17	A	B	C	A	D	A	D	A	A	B
18	B	A	A	C	D	C	C	D	A	A
19	D	A	D	D	B	B	D	C	B	C
20	C	C	B	B	A	D	B	D	C	D
21	C	B	A	C	B	C	D	B	A	B
22	B	A	C	C	B	D	C	C	B	B
23	A	B	D	A	C	A	A	A	C	A
24	C	D	B	D	A	B	A	D	C	D
25	A	C	D	B	D	A	B	D	D	C
26	C	A	C	A	B	C	D	A	D	C
27	B	C	A	C	C	B	C	A	A	B
28	D	B	B	A	A	D	D	D	B	C
29	A	D	D	D	D	B	A	B	C	C
30	D	A	C	B	B	A	B	C	C	A
31	A	D	C	C	B	B	A	D	A	D
32	C	D	D	A	A	C	C	C	B	D
33	B	A	D	D	C	A	D	A	A	A
34	D	B	A	B	C	D	B	C	C	C
35	B	C	B	D	D	B	C	B	D	B
36	D	B	A	D	A	C	B	D	A	D
37	A	D	C	A	C	A	C	B	D	B
38	C	A	B	B	D	B	A	C	B	B
39	B	D	C	B	D	C	B	C	C	B
40	B	D	D	C	B	C	B	B	D	C